LEARN THE LANGUAGE OF
THE INTERNET

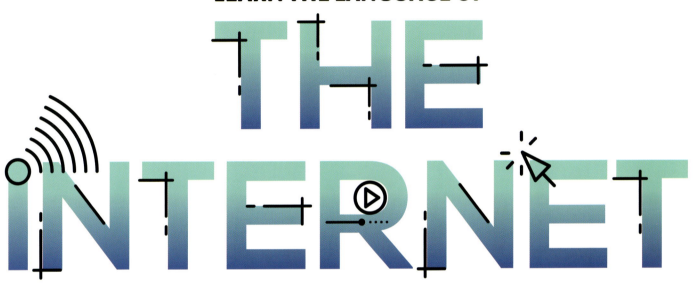

BY WILLIAM ANTHONY

BookLife PUBLISHING

©2019
BookLife Publishing Ltd.
King's Lynn
Norfolk, PE30 4LS

All rights reserved.
Printed in Malaysia.

A catalogue record for this book is available from the British Library.

ISBN: 978-1-78637-691-6

Written by:
William Anthony

Edited by:
Madeline Tyler

Designed by:
Dan Scase

All facts, statistics, web addresses and URLs in this book were verified as valid and accurate at time of writing.

No responsibility for any changes to external websites or references can be accepted by either the author or publisher.

Coventry City Council	
WHO*	
3 8002 02458 046 8	
Askews & Holts	Feb-2020
J004.678014 JUNIOR N	£12.99

PHOTO CREDITS

All images are courtesy of Shutterstock.com, unless otherwise specified. With thanks to Getty Images, Thinkstock Photo and iStockphoto.
Front Cover – Toria, Sergey Nivens. 4 – Alexander Lysenko, Astrovector, Finevector. 5 – tmicons, VectorsMarket, Solomonkein. 6 – Wit Olszewski. 7 – linear_design, svtdesign, Oakview Studios, l000s_pixels, premiumicon. 8 – NanamiOu, zo3listic, Ajay Shrivastava, Focus_Vector. 9 – dikobraziy, Siberian Art. 10 – Vladimir Kanuh, Blan-k. 11 – Flat_Enot , Meth Mehr. 12 – Lemonade Serenade. 13 – popicon, Fouaddesigns, Jane Kelly. 14 – Anatolir, Vita Stocker, SINWATTHANAWUT. 15 – MD. Delwar hossain, Design lover. 16 – Avector, Beatriz Gascon J. 17 – iconohek, CandyDuck, Vdant85. 18 – lukmanhakim, howcolour. 19 – Vector.design, ASAG Studio, Myvector. 20 – ZabVector, Ysami. 21 – Gal Csilla, LovArt. 22 – sundora14, T-Kot. 23 – Vector Icon Flat, Mehsumov. 24 – Fotos593. 25 – RRZ, nelelena, LANTERIA. 26 – Vector, Martial Red. 27 – por_suwat. 28 – Nobelus, Jane Kelly, WEB-DESIGN. 29 – Vitya_M, Yuriy Vlasenko. 30 – Daxiao Productions, a-image, MonsterDesign, tandaV, Andrey_Popov. 31 – Elvugar Karimli.

HOW TO DE:CODE THE LANGUAGE OF THE INTERNET

The internet is a huge digital world, and there are a whole host of strange and wonderful words that go along with it. This handy guide will help you learn them all – but first, let's take a look at how to De:Code each word.

METADATA
(MEH-TUH-DAY-TUH)

Noun: information hidden inside a web page to help search engines find it. It often includes a description of the page which will be recognised by search engines. See **SEO**.

HEADWORD: this shows you how a word is spelt. These words are organised in alphabetical order.

PRONUNCIATION GUIDE:
this tells you how to say a word out loud. Say each part exactly how it's written to pronounce the word correctly.

Word class: this is the type of word that the headword is. In this book you will see some of these:
- Noun – a person, place or thing
- Verb – an action word
- Adjective – a describing word

Abbreviations: this is the type of word that the headword is. In this book you may see some of these:
- Initialism – a set of letters taken from several words that are read as individual letters
- Acronym – a set of letters taken from several words that make a new word

Definition: this is what the headword means.

RELATED WORDS: this shows you other words that link to the one you're looking at.

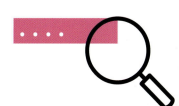

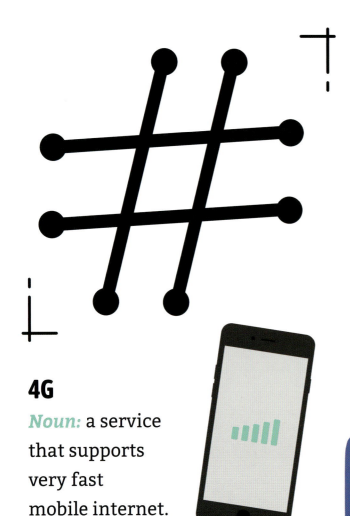

4G

Noun: a service that supports very fast mobile internet.

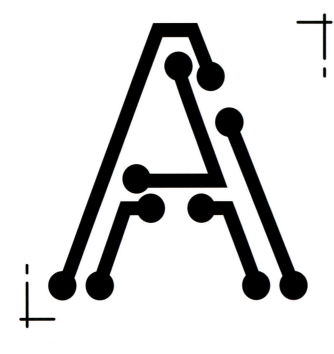

ACCOUNT

Noun: an online profile that is accessed by one person or a group of people.

ADDRESS BAR

Noun: the small section at the top of a browser in which you enter a URL. See **BROWSER** and **URL**.

http://www.

ADVERTISING

Noun: a way that businesses show off their products or services. This can be in the form of videos or images.

ANTIVIRUS PROTECTION (AN-TEE-VY-RUS PRO-TEK-SHUN)

Noun: software that helps to keep your computer, and the information stored on it, safe.

APP

Noun: short for application. An app is a program installed and used on a computer system or portable device. Types of app include games, internet browsers and social media sites. See **BROWSER**.

ATTACHMENT

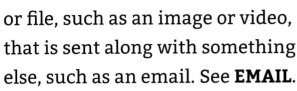

Noun: a document or file, such as an image or video, that is sent along with something else, such as an email. See **EMAIL**.

AUTHENTICITY
(ORTH-EN-TIH-CITY)

Noun: how real an online account is. If you don't think an account looks like a real person has made it, you should probably stay away from it. See **PHISHING.**

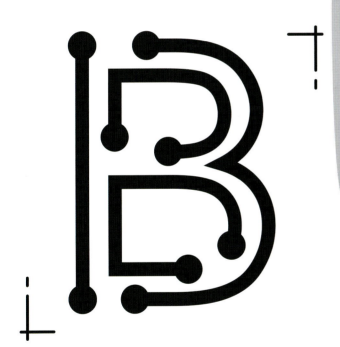

BAN

Noun: a period of time that a user is not allowed access to their account. A website might give a ban out to a user that has been behaving in a bad way online. This can be thought of as a time-out.

BANDWIDTH

Noun: how much data can be sent at once. Imagine two hoses, one thin and one thick. Both deliver water, but the bigger hose delivers more water at once – this is similar to how bandwidth works. The more bandwidth a connection has, the more data it can send and receive at one time. See **DATA**.

BASKET

Noun: a virtual shopping basket in an online shop that you add your items to. This lets you buy all the items you want at once, instead of paying for each thing separately.

BETA
(BAY-TUH)

Noun: a version of a website, app or game that is nearly complete. It is open to a small number of users to find bugs or problems before it goes live.

BINGE-WATCHING

Verb: watching lots of videos or TV episodes in a row for very long periods of time without stopping.

BITCOIN

Noun: a type of digital money, called cryptocurrency, that can be used in the same way as real money to buy things on the internet or to transfer to other people. See **CRYPTOCURRENCY**.

BLOG

Noun: a website on which a blogger uploads regular pieces of content about a topic. This word is created from combining 'web' and 'log'.

BOOKMARKING

Verb: saving something you found important, enjoyed, or want to continue reading later.

BUFFERING

Verb: downloading a certain amount of data before starting to play some music or a movie.

BOT

Noun: a program that is made to behave like a real person online and can interact with a system or user.

BROWSER

Noun: a computer program that is used to find and look at information on the internet.

BUG

Noun: an error in a piece of software that stops it from working the way that it should do.

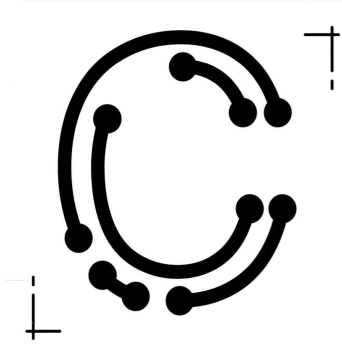

CLICKBAIT

Noun: a title or advert made to look so interesting that lots of people click on it. The web page it links to usually has very little to do with the title or advert that you clicked on.

CACHE (CASH)

Noun: a place where computers can store recently used information so that it can be accessed quickly the next time that it's needed.

CLOUD

Noun: the large computers, called servers, that you can connect to on the internet and use for storing data.

COMMENT

Noun: a response that is often provided as an answer or reaction to a blog post or a post on a social network.

COOKIES

Noun: small pieces of information that a website creates to remember things about you. These can be your username and password, or which type of pages you like to look at most.

CAPTCHA

Noun: a computer program that can tell whether a human or a machine is entering information into a website. This can involve copying out the letters you see in an image, like the one below. Normally, these are used at the end of online forms. See **FORM**.

CROWDFUNDING

Verb: raising money online for new and unique products to be made.

CRYPTOCURRENCY

Noun: digital currency (a type of money) that uses encryption to keep it safe and secure. It is not controlled by a government like real-life money. See **ENCRYPTION**.

CSS (Cascading Style Sheets)

Initialism: a set of instructions to describe the formatting (for example, the layout, font and size) of a document, written in a computer language such as HTML. See **HTML**.

CYBERBULLYING (SIGH-BUR-BULLY-ING)

Verb: doing something cruel on the internet, usually again and again, to make another person feel angry, sad or scared.

If you are being bullied online, always tell an adult that you trust about it. You can also visit websites such as **https://www.bullying.co.uk/cyberbullying/, https://www.connectsafely.org/tips-to-help-stop-cyberbullying/** *and* **https://www.childline.org.uk/get-support/** *for advice and support.*

WORD JUMBLE

Each group of letters below is a jumbled up word from this book. Can you rearrange the letters and figure out what each word is? If you're finding it a bit tricky, why not flick through the book to check out some of the words that might be jumbled.

1. FSINRGU

2. EOKRTNW

3. KSEOICO

4. YIPRCVA

5. AIFCTFR

6. MTATHANCTE

7. OLGV

8. ITINBOC

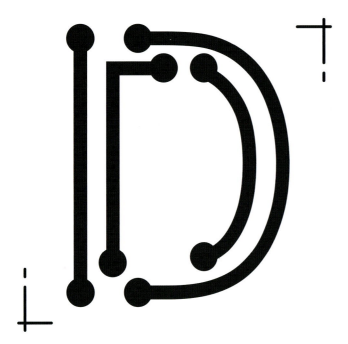

DATA

Noun: information that can be understood by a computer, such as text, images and videos.

DEACTIVATE

Verb: to close an online account. Sometimes the deleted account can be reopened, and other times it is deleted forever. Always check before you close your account in case you want to reopen it again in the future.

DEVELOPER

Noun: someone who is involved in coding, programming or designing a website.

DIAL-UP

Noun: a way of connecting to the internet back in the 1990s and 2000s, which made strange beeping noises as it loaded.

DIGITAL FOOTPRINT

Noun: the information, sometimes personal, left by someone on the internet.

DOMAIN NAME

Noun: the letters, numbers and punctuation that make up the main part of a URL. For example, in 'www.decode.com/the-internet', 'www.decode.com' would be the domain name. See **URL**.

DOWNLOAD

Verb: to copy data from one computer system to another, usually across the internet.

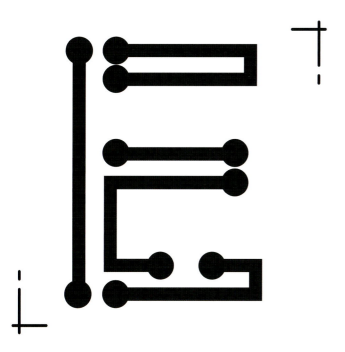

eCOMMERCE
(EE-COM-MURSE)
Noun: the electronic buying and selling of a product or service online, such as on shopping websites.

EGOSURFING
(EE-GO-SUR-FING)
Verb: browsing the internet for a mention of yourself to make you feel important.

EMAIL
Noun: electronic messages that can be sent from one device to another over the internet.

eBOOK
Noun: an electronic version of a book.

ENCRYPTION
(EN-CRIP-SHUN)
Noun: a way of changing and scrambling information so that it can't be read by anyone who doesn't know the password or key to unscramble it. This makes the information safer.

ENGAGEMENT
Noun: the amount that users interact with a particular website, profile or post.

#ABCDEFGHIJKLMNOPQRSTUVWXYZ

DE:CODE

404. That's an error.

The requested URL /error was not found on this server.
That's all we know. Sorry.

ERROR 404

Noun: a message displayed by your internet browser that means it is unable to find the web page you are looking for. Please try again soon. See **BROWSER**.

ETHERNET CABLE
(EE-THER-NET CAY-BUL)

Noun: a wire used to connect devices to each other or to the internet. If your Wi-Fi connection isn't working and you need to access the internet, you might have to use an ethernet cable to connect your computer to your router. See **ROUTER**.

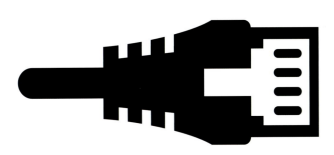

eZINE

Noun: an online magazine.

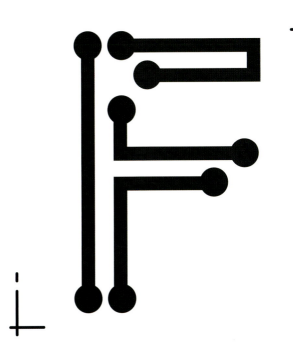

FAKE NEWS

Noun: false stories that look like real news and are spread on the internet, usually created to influence people's opinions or as a joke. It is important to not always believe what you read – except this book. This book tells you the truth.

FAQ
(Frequently Asked Questions)

Initialism: a list of answers to commonly asked questions. Reading these might save people the time it takes to get in contact with a website or company.

FILE NOT FOUND

Noun: a message that means your computer or web browser can't find the file that you've asked it to look for. This is usually a sad time. See **BROWSER**.

A B C D E F G H I J K L M N O P Q R S T U V W X Y Z

FILTER

Noun: software that prevents someone from looking at certain things on the internet.

FIREWALL

Noun: hardware or software that controls what information passes from your computer to the internet, and who or what can access your computer while you're connected. DO NOT try to make a wall of fire in real life. That would be dangerous.

FLASH

Noun: a plug-in used to create and play interactive videos, games and other multimedia items on the internet. See **PLUG-IN**.

FLIGHT TRACKER

Noun: an online service that provides you with real-time information about thousands of aircraft and flights around the world.

FORM

Noun: an online document with blank spaces for filling in information.

FORUM

Noun: an online discussion site on which people talk about specific topics in a thread. Also known as a message board. See **THREAD**.

FREEZE

Verb: when a website stops loading, moving or working correctly. Try refreshing the page to correct a frozen website. See **REFRESH**.

GOOGLING

Verb: searching for something using Google. See **SEARCH ENGINE**.

HISTORY

Noun: a log of the websites you have visited on your browser. You can usually clear or delete this. See **BROWSER**.

HOMEPAGE

Noun: the web page your browser automatically displays when you start it up, or the main page of a website. See **BROWSER**.

HOTSPOT

Noun: an area in which you can connect to a wireless internet connection.

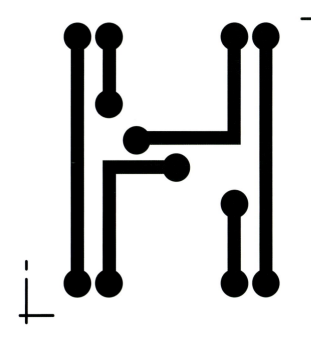

HACK

Verb: to attempt to access someone's personal information without their permission, or harm a person's computer or system, over the internet.

A B C D E F **G** H I J K L M N O P Q R S T U V W X Y Z

\# A B C D E F G H I J K L M N O P Q R S T U V W X Y Z

HTML (Hypertext Markup Language)

Initialism: one of the first coding languages designed to be used for formatting web pages.

HTTP (Hypertext Transfer Protocol)

Initialism: a set of rules for transferring files and messages on the World Wide Web. HTTPS is a more secure version of this. See **WORLD WIDE WEB.**

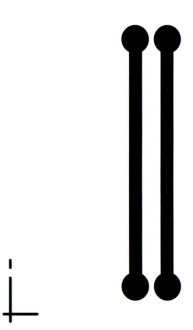

INBOX

Noun: a folder that holds new email messages. See **EMAIL.**

INTERNET OF THINGS

Noun: the way that everyday objects are all connected over the internet.

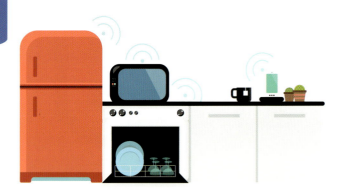

IP ADDRESS

Noun: a number assigned to any device that is connected to the internet, which will look something like '01.234.56.789'. It helps to locate where in the world the device is.

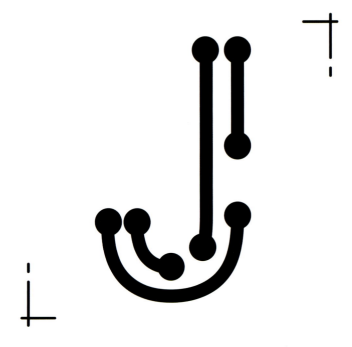

JOIN

Verb: to add yourself to, or become part of, a group or website.

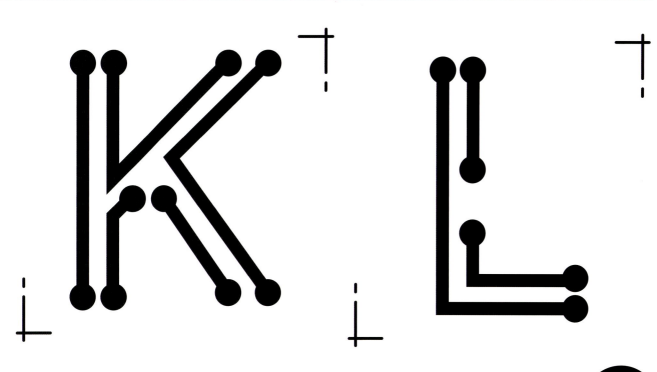

KEEP ME LOGGED IN

Noun: usually a tick box that, if clicked, will stop you from having to enter your details and password every time you enter the website. If you share a computer or device, it might be best to sign in and out every time.

LINK

Noun: a virtual bridge from one website to another, to direct people somewhere, or to allow information to be shared.

LURKER

Noun: someone who visits and reads forums but doesn't post anything.

KEYBOARD WARRIOR
(KEE-BORD WOR-REE-UH)

Noun: someone who only has arguments online rather than in real life.

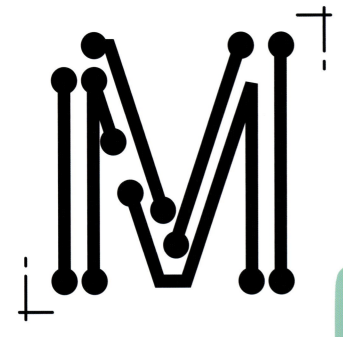

METADATA
(MEH-TUH-DAY-TUH)

Noun: information hidden inside a web page to help search engines find it. It often includes a description of the page that will be recognised by search engines. See **SEO**.

MALWARE

Noun: harmful software designed to mess with the normal operation of a computer.

MODERATOR

Noun: someone who is in charge of a forum, website or group conversation and has the ability to edit it however they wish. They can also take action against bad or inappropriate behaviour by blocking or removing people.

MEDIA

Noun: ways of communicating information. This could be through writing, photos, videos or audio, among others.

MOUSE POTATO

Noun: someone who spends most of their day at a computer.

MULTIMEDIA

Noun: combinations of text, graphics, video, animation and/or sound. See **MEDIA**.

MENU

Noun: a list of available options. Unfortunately, there's no food to be found here.

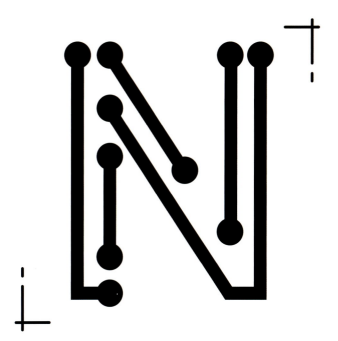
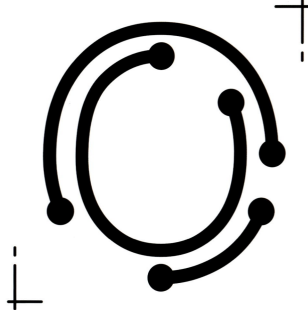

NAVIGATION BAR

Noun: a menu of buttons that link to important or big sections of a website. See **MENU**.

NETIQUETTE
(NET-IH-KET)

Noun: polite behaviour on the internet. For example, typing everything in capital letters is thought to be like shouting, WHICH IS NOT GOOD NETIQUETTE!!!

NETWORK

Noun: computers and devices within a building or area that are linked together.

OFFLINE

Adjective: when your device isn't connected to the internet. If this isn't on purpose, it can be rather frustrating when you're desperate to upload that selfie.

ON DEMAND

Noun: TV programmes or films that are available to be watched online whenever the viewer wants to watch them.

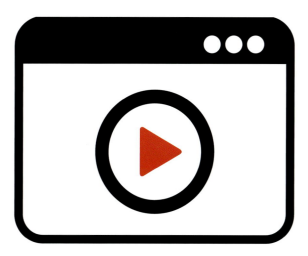

A B C D E F G H I J K L M N O P Q R S T U V W X Y Z

ONLINE

Adjective: when your device is connected to the internet, and the World Wide Web is ready at your fingertips. See **WORLD WIDE WEB**.

OUTBOX

Noun: a folder that holds emails that are waiting to be sent to other people.

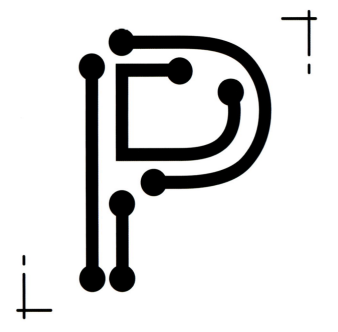

PASSWORD

Noun: a secret combination of letters and numbers (and sometimes other characters) that protects personal information.

How To Choose a Strong Password

- Use at least eight characters
- Use upper- and lower-case letters
- Use symbols and numbers
- Don't use easy combinations like '12345678'

PHARMING (FAR-MING)

Verb: using a piece of malware to redirect people to websites that look a lot like the real thing but are fake. They are designed to infect computers with viruses, take personal data or scam people into giving away money. See **MALWARE.**

PHISHING (FISH-ING)

Verb: attempting to get personal information such as usernames and passwords over the internet by pretending to be a company or a different person. See **AUTHENTICITY**.

PLUG-IN

Noun: an extra bit of software code, such as Flash, that needs to be added to your browser before you can view or use certain types of content. See **FLASH**.

PODCAST

Noun: a series of audio files or videos in which presenters talk about and discuss different topics.

POP-UP

Noun: an extra browser window that appears from nowhere. These can be good (such as prompts from your social media account telling you to log off) or bad (such as adverts and spam). See **BROWSER**.

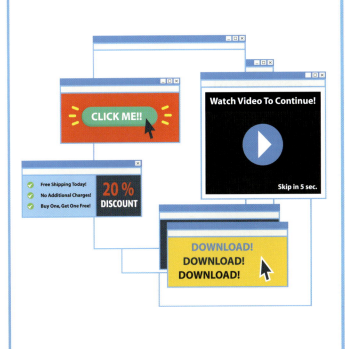

PORTAL

Noun: a page on the internet full of links to and information about other web pages, with very little content of its own. This is definitely NOT something that takes you to a different dimension.

PRIVACY

Noun: settings for social media accounts that determine how much of your account can be seen by the public or by your friends or followers. You should change these settings so that your account can't be seen by people you aren't friends with or who don't follow you.

PRIVATE BROWSER

Noun: a window that can be opened in your web browser that doesn't allow cookies and doesn't track your history.

PUSH NOTIFICATION

Noun: an automatic message sent to your computer, tablet or smartphone by an app, even when the app isn't open. See **APP**.

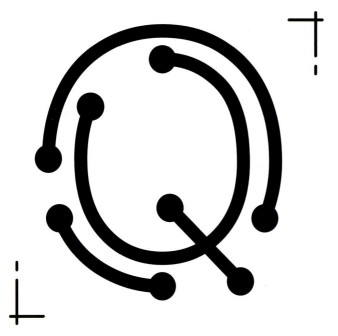

RATING

Noun: a way people review or measure how good something is. This might be done with stars out of five, or marks out of ten. For example, this book is almost certainly worth a five-star rating! See **REVIEW**.

QR CODE

Noun: a square with lots of smaller square and rectangular shapes inside that can be scanned by a device and used to launch a website.

REFRESH

Verb: to force a web page to load again. Useful in those annoying moments when your website has frozen and doesn't work properly. See **FREEZE**.

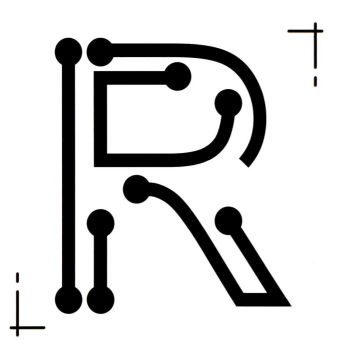

RESTRICTED

Adjective: something that is hidden from certain users, usually those under the age of 18.

A B C D E F G H I J K L M N O P Q R S T U V W X Y Z

REVIEW

Noun: a report in which someone gives their opinion about a product, topic or website. Sometimes this comes with a rating. See **RATING**.

RIGHT-CLICK

Verb: pressing the button on the right of some mice or trackpads in order to open a menu. The menu is related to the thing you have clicked on.

ROAMING

Verb: connecting to an internet service while you are away from home and not connected to Wi-Fi. Some mobile phone networks will let you roam while you are in another country. See **WI-FI**.

ROUTER
(ROO-TUH)

Noun: a piece of hardware that directs wireless signals, such as an internet connection, to other electronic devices. Try turning this off and on again if your internet signal has stopped. See **WI-FI**.

WORD RUSH

There are a lot of words in this book, but how many of them can you make from these letters in just 2 minutes? You can use each letter square just once for each word. Play on your own or grab a friend to challenge. Find a pen, get some paper and start the timer! 3... 2... 1...

W	T	U	O	N	F
G	S	A	A	Z	B
U	H	P	R	E	D
V	N	Y	M	O	E
A	D	W	J	R	I
M	F	S	C	B	T

SAFETY

Noun: being away from harm or danger. The internet might not seem like a dangerous place, but it is similar to the outside world. A lot of it is full of good people using it for good things, but there are some bad people who use it for bad things.

Tip:
Try to use strong passwords to keep your accounts safe, stay away from websites that don't seem trustworthy, and don't follow accounts on social media that don't look like a real person has made them. See **PASSWORD** and **AUTHENTICITY**.

SEARCH ENGINE

Noun: a program that searches for items that include chosen keywords or characters in a database.

SEO (Search Engine Optimisation)

Initialism: the use of different types of information in a web page to get it to the top of the list of results in a search engine.

SOCIAL MEDIA

Noun: websites on which people can create online accounts and communities where they can share information or messages. See **ACCOUNT**.

SPAM EMAIL

Noun: unwanted emails, usually from businesses and advertisers.

SPEED TEST

Noun: a way of finding out how fast your internet is.

STREAMING

Verb: watching a video file or listening to a music file at almost the same time that it is being downloaded by your computer. This way, you don't have to wait for it to be downloaded first.

SURFING

Verb: jumping from website to website. You aren't riding any waves while you do this.

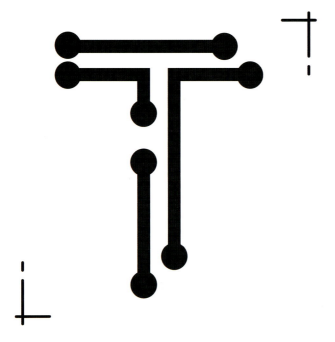

TABS

Noun: separate web page windows that are open in your browser at any one time. See **BROWSER**.

TERMS & CONDITIONS

Noun: a set of rules that you must agree to follow before you use certain websites. If you don't follow these rules, you could end up being banned from the website!

TETHERING
(TEH-THE-RING)

Noun: the linking of one device to another in order to share an internet connection.

THREAD

Noun: a series of messages or posts on the same topic on a social media platform. These can represent real-life conversations.

TRAFFIC

Noun: the number of visitors a website gets. Just like on busy city roads, more traffic slows down a website.

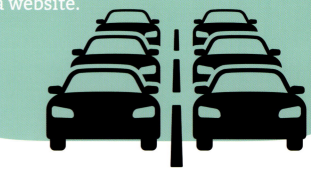

TRENDING

Verb: to be one of the most talked-about or viewed pages on a particular website.

TROJAN

Noun: a program that appears harmless but is carrying viruses or even other programs within it that will damage a computer or allow someone to hack into it. See **HACK**.

TROLL

Noun: a person who creates controversy on the internet. Trolls are known for disrupting conversations online to get angry reactions from other users or to make them feel sad.

If someone is trolling you online, there are a few things you should do:
• Report the troll's account to the website that you're using.
• Ignore their comments and do not reply. It might be very difficult to ignore the troll, but you should

TRUSTWORTHY WEBSITE

Noun: a website that can be relied on to be honest and truthful.

not reply to them. Trolls are looking for reactions, so don't give them one.
• Take a break away from the website. If other users on the website are upsetting you, it's good to simply leave it alone for a while.
• Speak to someone! Above all, talking to an adult about how the comments are making you feel will help you a lot.

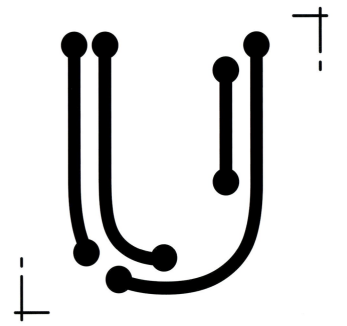

URL (Uniform Resource Locator)

Initialism: a website address.

USER-FRIENDLY

Adjective: a type of program that is built in an easy-to-use way.

USER-GENERATED CONTENT

Noun: information or media created for the internet by the people that use it. This might be in the form of videos, blogs, photos and much more.

UPLOAD

Verb: to post something on the internet. You should always be certain that you want to upload something before you make it visible to the world.

USERNAME

Noun: a name you give yourself to log in to accounts, which you can choose yourself and does not need to be your own name.

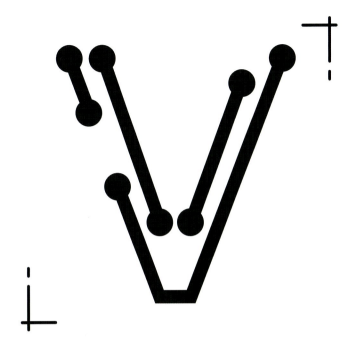

VIRUS

Noun: a type of malware that multiplies to spread across multiple computers and affects how they perform. See **MALWARE**.

VIRTUAL
(VUR-CHOO-UL)

Adjective: existing on computers or on the internet as a simulation of real life.

VISITORS

Noun: people who visit or view a particular website. The more visitors a website gets, the more successful it is.

VIDEO CALL

Noun: a type of call that allows you to see the other person or people through their camera.

VIRAL

Adjective: content that has spread across social media platforms very quickly by many users interacting with it. Not related to diseases.

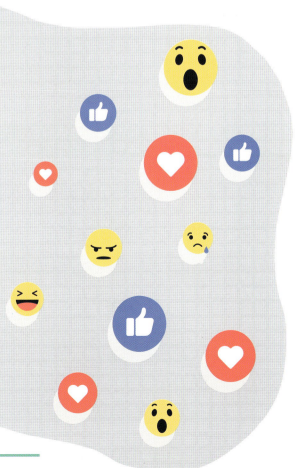

A B C D E F G H I J K L M N O P Q R S T U V W X Y Z

Search 🔍

Up next

CLICKBAIT: MORE THAN 99% OF PEOPLE CAN'T GUESS WHAT THIS WORD MEANS!
Turn to page 8 to find out!

AUTOPLAY

WORLD WIDE WEB
BookLife Publishing Ltd ✔
22K views
Page 31

TRUSTWORTHY WEBSITE
BookLife Publishing Ltd ✔
225K views
Page 27

PUSH NOTIFICATION
BookLife Publishing Ltd ✔
372K views
Page 21

CROWDFUNDING
BookLife Publishing Ltd ✔
95K views
Page 9

👍 60K 👎 0 SHARE SAVE •••

JOIN **SUBSCRIBE 7.9M**

VLOG

BookLife Publishing Ltd ✔
Published on June 28th 2019

Noun: video content created to record the events in someone's life for the entertainment of others. These are normally uploaded to social media websites. The word 'vlog' is created from the words 'video log'.

SHOW MORE

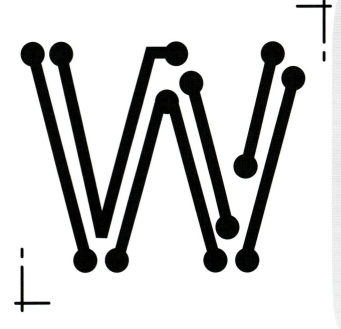

WORLD WIDE WEB

Noun: a collection of web pages found on the internet.

WEBCAM

Noun: a small camera either built into, or that can be plugged into, your computer so that you can see and talk to people over the internet. You should only use a webcam to talk to people you know. See **VIDEO CALL**.

WEBSITE

Noun: a collection of web pages that all link together under a single domain name. See **DOMAIN NAME**.

WI-FI
(WHY-FY)

Noun: a facility that lets computers, smartphones, or other devices connect to the internet.

WIKI
(WIH-KEE)

Noun: a type of website that is developed by its community of users. Users can add or edit the content on it. See **USER-GENERATED CONTENT**.

ZOMBIE COMPUTER

Noun: a computer that someone has hacked into over the internet and can be used to do whatever the hacker wants without the owner noticing.

WORD MATCH

Now that you've learned all of the words in this book, can you match them up to the correct definitions? Try to complete them all without looking back at the rest of the book!

TERMS

- 4G
- DEVELOPER
- ENGAGEMENT
- HACK
- PUSH NOTIFICATION
- JOIN
- OUTBOX
- RESTRICTED
- TRENDING
- BROWSER
- TRUSTWORTHY WEBSITE
- eZINE

DEFINITIONS

- a computer program that is used to find and look at information on the internet
- a service that supports very fast mobile internet
- something that is hidden from certain users, usually those under the age of 18
- the amount that users interact with a particular website, profile or post
- an online magazine
- someone who is involved in coding, programming or designing a website
- to add yourself to, or become part of, a group or website
- a folder that holds email messages that are waiting to send to other people
- an automatic message sent to your computer, tablet or smartphone by an app, even when the app isn't open
- a website that can be relied on to be honest and truthful
- to attempt to access someone's personal information without their permission, or harm a person's computer or system, over the internet
- to be one of the most talked-about or viewed pages on a particular website